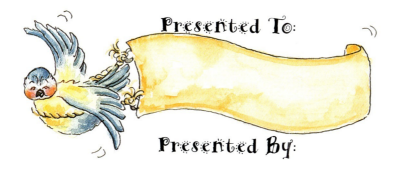

Presented To:

Presented By:

_____

Date:

_____

God's Little Story Book of Bible Heroes

Tulsa, Oklahoma

Stories based on the following Bible versions:

The Holy Bible, New International Version®. NIV®. Copyright © 1973, 1978, 1984 by International Bible Society. Used by permission of Zondervan Publishing House. All rights reserved.

The *King James Version* of the Bible.

God's Little Story Book of Bible Heroes
ISBN 1-56292-000-6
Copyright © 2001 by Honor Books
P.O. Box 55388
Tulsa, OK 74155

Printed in the United States of America. All rights reserved under International Copyright Law. Contents and/or cover may not be reproduced in whole or in part in any form without the express written consent of the Publisher.

Written by Sarah M. Hupp
Cover and Interior Design by Whisner Design Group
Illustrated by Lisa Browning

introduction

God's Little Story Book of Bible Heroes tells the stories of great men and women who did amazing things for God. Some of them were young, and some of them were old. Some of them were short, and some of them were tall. Some of them were scared, but all of them were brave. They were people just like you.

Joseph was a little brother who dreamed he would one day do great things. It made his brothers mad. But his dreams came true. Deborah loved God with all her heart. People came to her for help—even a great soldier. David also loved God with all his heart. He took care of the sheep before he was made king. And another of the Bible's heroes is a little boy who gave Jesus his lunch. Jesus took it and fed thousands of people. It was a miracle!

Read these stories and learn how God helped ordinary people become heroes. God loves you just as much. He will help you grow up and do great things too. Come on . . . let's read!

Contents

God's Promise to Abram 9

Joseph Has a Dream 13

God Gives the Law 16

Joshua's Faith 20

Rahab Helps the Spies 24

Deborah Rules Wisely 29

Not Big, but Brave 33

The Strongest Man in the World 36

David Honors God 40

David and Goliath 45

A Wise Decision 49

Elijah and the Widow 52

Wind and Fire 57

Here I Am, Send Me!	61
Fifteen More Years	65
A Young King Makes a Difference	68
The Writing on the Wall	72
Esther Saves Her People	77
John the Baptist	81
A New Job for Matthew	85
A Roman Commander Has Faith	88
A Boy Gives His Lunch Away	92
Peter Walks on Water	96
A Brave Believer	101
You Can Stay with Us	104
Just Like a Son	109

God's Promise to Abram

(Genesis 12:1-7; 15:5-18)

Long, long ago, God spoke to a man named Abram. God said, "I want you to go to a new country. I will bless you and make you a great nation. You will be a blessing to many people." So Abram started walking.

Abram walked and walked. Finally God said, "Stop! This is where I want you and your family to live!" So Abram stopped. Then God said, "Look up at the stars. Try to count them. That is how many children and grandchildren you will have!"

When Abram looked up, he saw more stars than he could count. But Abram believed that God would keep His promise.

Dear God, help me to trust You and believe Your promises as Abram did. Amen.

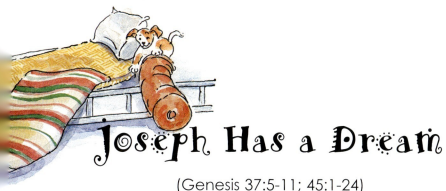

Joseph Has a Dream

(Genesis 37:5-11; 45:1-24)

One morning, Joseph jumped out of bed. He ran to find his brothers. "I want to tell you something," he said. Joseph's brothers didn't want to listen. But Joseph kept talking.

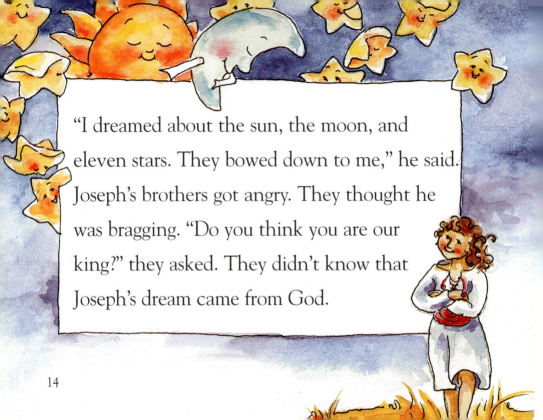

"I dreamed about the sun, the moon, and eleven stars. They bowed down to me," he said. Joseph's brothers got angry. They thought he was bragging. "Do you think you are our king?" they asked. They didn't know that Joseph's dream came from God.

Many years later, during a time of great hunger, Joseph became a powerful ruler. He fed the people. Everyone bowed down to him. Joseph's brothers bowed down to him too. God made Joseph's dream come true.

Dear God, You had good plans for Joseph. Thank You that You have good plans for me too. Amen.

God Gives the Law

(Exodus 34:1–35)

God told Moses to cut two tablets out of stone. God said He would write His laws on the tablets. So Moses went up on the mountain. He carried the stone tablets in his hands. He did everything God said.

God came down on top of the mountain in a cloud. He talked with Moses, and Moses worshipped Him. God wrote His laws on the stone tablets with His finger. Those laws are called the Ten Commandments.

Moses stayed on the mountain for forty days. He talked with God every day. And his face glowed because he talked to God.

Dear God, I want to be Your friend and talk to You every day just as Moses did. Amen.

Joshua's Faith

(Numbers 13; Deuteronomy 1:19-25; 1:38)

God wanted twelve men to go into the Promised Land and look around. So Joshua and eleven other men went. They were gone for a long time. When they came back, they were excited. The land was beautiful!

There were good things to eat, too, like milk, honey, and grapes. But ten of the men said there was a big problem. They said, "The people in the land are too strong for us. We can't fight them."

But Joshua said, "God is more powerful than anyone. He will help us." Because Joshua's faith in God was strong, he finally became the leader of God's people.

Dear God, help me to have a strong faith in You as Joshua did. Amen.

Rahab Helps the Spies

(Joshua 2)

God's people moved into the land of Canaan. They sent two men into the city of Jericho to look around. The men came to Rahab's house. She told them about her city. She told them about the people who lived there too.

The king of Jericho heard that two spies were at Rahab's house. So the king sent soldiers to capture the two men. But Rahab hid the men on her rooftop under some straw. The soldiers never found them.

The men were so thankful! They gave their word that God's people would be kind to Rahab. Then the men escaped with Rahab's help.

Thank You, God, for Rahab's kindness. Help me to be kind to others too. Amen.

Deborah Rules Wisely

(Judges 4–5)

Deborah loved and honored God. She spoke God's words to the people. She told them to follow God's commands. Deborah was wise too. Many people asked Deborah for advice when they had a problem.

The king of Canaan was mean to God's people. So Deborah told one of God's soldiers to go and fight the king. She said God would be with him. But the soldier was afraid. He refused to fight unless Deborah went with him.

Deborah was brave. She helped fight the bad king. So God's people won the battle. Then Deborah praised God for always helping her.

Dear God, help me to be like Deborah and praise You for everything too.
Amen.

Not Big, but Brave

(Judges 6, 7)

The king of Midian was really mean to God's people. So God sent an angel to a young man named Gideon. The angel said, "God will use you to save God's people. You are a mighty man."

Could the angel's message be true? Gideon wasn't sure. So he asked God to prove it. He asked God to make a sheepskin wet but leave the ground around it dry. God did it!

Then Gideon asked God to make the sheepskin dry but the ground wet. God did that too. Because God answered Gideon's prayers, Gideon believed the angel's message. He believed that God would help him save His people. And God did.

Thank You, God, for answering my prayers and making me brave like Gideon. Amen.

The Strongest Man in the World

(Judges 13–16)

Samson's parents wanted him to serve God. They told God that Samson would never get a haircut. So God gave Samson a gift in return. God made him strong. But Samson didn't use his strength wisely. That made people angry.

One woman learned the secret of Samson's strength. So while Samson was sleeping, she cut his hair. Samson's strength was gone! His enemies trapped him, poked out his eyes, and put him in prison.

While he was in prison, Samson's hair grew back.
And God made Samson strong once more—strong
enough to push over the temple of the Philistines.

*Thank You, God, for the gifts You have given me.
Help me to use them wisely. Amen.*

David Honors God

(1 Samuel 16)

David loved God very much. He thought about God all the time. He thought about God as he took care of his father's sheep. He thought about God when he looked at the sky. The grass and the trees and the birds and the bees reminded him of God.

The sheep listened when David played his harp. He sang songs to God. Many people heard David's songs. Some of them were written down. You can find them in the Bible in the book of Psalms.

David was "dear to God's own heart." When David grew up, God chose him to be the second king of Israel.

I love you, God! I'm glad you are happy when I honor you as David did. Amen.

David and Goliath

(1 Samuel 17:17-50)

One day, David's father told him to take food to his big brothers. They were in God's army. David was so excited! He was just a little shepherd boy. When David got to camp, he heard a big, mean giant say bad things about God and His people.

The giant said he would kill anyone who tried to fight him. David said to the giant, "I will fight you in God's name. My God is stronger than you."

That made the giant angry! David put a small stone in his slingshot and threw it right at the giant's head. The giant fell down dead. David was a hero!

Dear Lord, help me to be brave like David. Help me to tell others how strong You are. Amen.

A Wise Decision

(1 Kings 3)

God made Solomon king of Israel. God told Solomon to ask Him for anything. Solomon asked God to make him wise. So God made Solomon the wisest man in the world.

Once two mothers came to Solomon. They lived in the same house and had babies who were the same age. One night one of the babies died. Each mother said that the living baby was hers.

Someone was lying!

Solomon told a soldier to cut the baby in half. But one mother cried, "Don't hurt the baby!" Then Solomon knew that she was the baby's real mother.

Dear God, please help me to make wise choices too. Amen.

Elijah and the Widow

(1 Kings 17)

Elijah told lots of people about God. He told people in the city. He told people in the country. One day Elijah met a woman. He asked her for some food. But the woman said she only had enough flour and oil to make one little piece of bread.

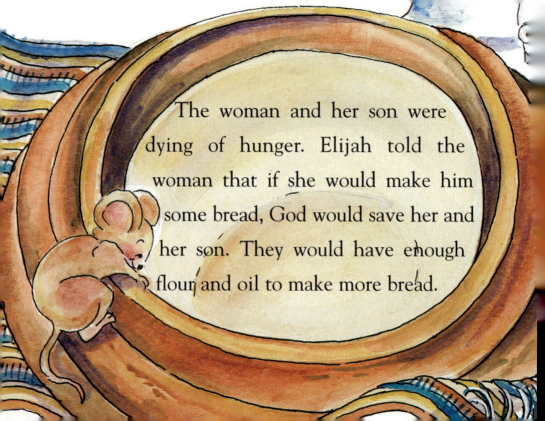

The woman and her son were dying of hunger. Elijah told the woman that if she would make him some bread, God would save her and her son. They would have enough flour and oil to make more bread.

So the woman baked the bread for Elijah.
And God did a miracle. The woman's flour
and oil jars were never empty again.

*Thank You, God, for taking care of the woman
and her son and for taking care of me too.
Amen.*

Wind and Fire

(2 Kings 2)

Elijah had a helper named Elisha. When Elijah was an old man, he knew it was time for him to go to heaven. Elisha wanted to have God's power like Elijah did. He asked Elijah what to do.

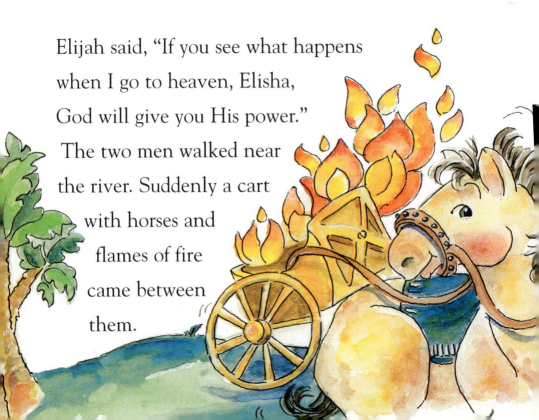

Elijah said, "If you see what happens when I go to heaven, Elisha, God will give you His power." The two men walked near the river. Suddenly a cart with horses and flames of fire came between them.

Then a great spinning wind lifted Elijah into heaven! Elisha watched until he couldn't see Elijah any more. Elisha had God's power from that day on.

Dear Lord, please give me Your power to do what You want me to do. Amen.

Here I Am, Send Me!

(Isaiah 6)

One day Isaiah had a vision of God's throne in heaven. In the vision, God looked great and glorious. But Isaiah felt small and sinful. Then an angel touched Isaiah's lips with a burning coal. God forgave Isaiah!

In Isaiah's vision, God asked who would go and speak God's words to the people. Isaiah cried, "Here I am! Send me!" God smiled at him. It was wonderful!

From that day on, Isaiah told everyone to follow God. And God blessed Isaiah for always telling people the truth about Him.

Dear God, help me to tell others about You just as Isaiah did. Amen.

Fifteen More Years

(2 Kings 20)

King Hezekiah was sick. No one knew how to make him feel better. Isaiah came and told him that he would die. Hezekiah cried out to God and prayed.

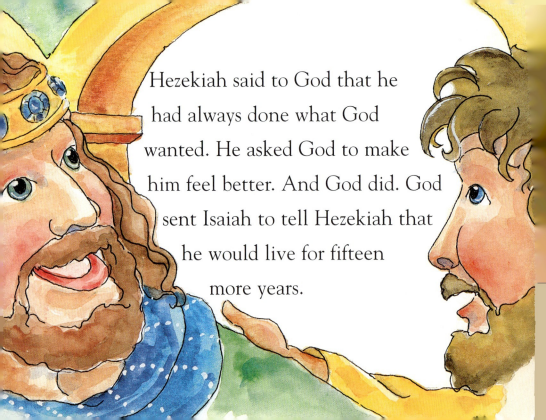

Hezekiah said to God that he had always done what God wanted. He asked God to make him feel better. And God did. God sent Isaiah to tell Hezekiah that he would live for fifteen more years.

Hezekiah was happy! In three days Hezekiah felt better and went to the temple to honor God for making him feel better.

Dear God, thank You for hearing my prayers too. Amen.

A Young King Makes a Difference

(2 Kings 22–23)

Josiah was only eight years old when he became the king of Israel. He was a good king who loved God. Josiah saw that God's house was falling down. So Josiah asked people to come and fix God's temple.

While the people were working, someone found a book in God's house. It was God's Law! And it made Josiah sad. He knew that his people were not living the way God wanted them to.

So Josiah made things different in Israel. He told everyone to do what God wanted. God blessed Israel because Josiah followed God with all his heart.

I love You, God! Help me to follow You always as Josiah did. Amen.

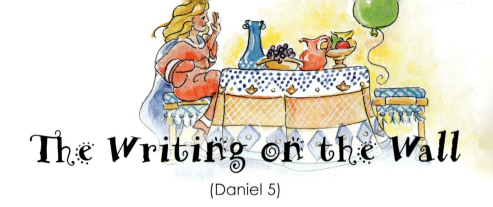

The Writing on the Wall

(Daniel 5)

Belshazzar was the proud king of Babylon. One day Belshazzar gave a big party. He and his friends made fun of God. Suddenly, the fingers of a man's hand appeared and wrote strange words on the wall.

73

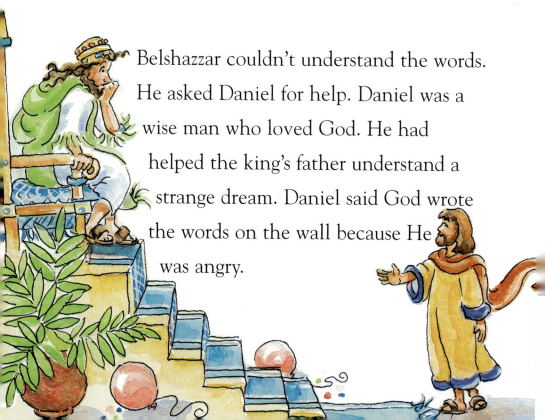

Belshazzar couldn't understand the words. He asked Daniel for help. Daniel was a wise man who loved God. He had helped the king's father understand a strange dream. Daniel said God wrote the words on the wall because He was angry.

Daniel said God would punish Belshazzar. He said God would take his kingdom away. That night Belshazzar was slain. Daniel became a leader in Babylon because he faithfully followed God.

Dear God, help me to be faithful to You as Daniel was. Amen.

Esther Saves Her People

(Esther 3–8)

King Xerxes of Persia signed a law. It said everyone had to bow down to his leaders. If people refused, they would be killed. But Queen Esther and God's people would not bow down to the king's leaders. They would only worship God.

Mordecai, one of God's people, asked Esther for help. So Esther gave two parties to honor the king. At the second party, the king asked Esther what she wanted in return for her kindness. Esther was scared. But she bravely asked the king to save her people.

So King Xerxes made another law to protect God's people. Esther's bravery and kindness helped save them all.

Dear God, please remind me to be brave and kind whenever I have a scary problem.
Amen.

John the Baptist

(Matthew 3)

John lived in the desert of Judea near a river. He wore strange clothes and ate strange food. He told people to turn away from their sinful ways.

Many people came to hear this strange man. They called him "John the Baptist". John said he baptized people's bodies with water. But one day, he said, God would baptize people's hearts with the Holy Spirit.

Jesus came to be baptized by him. John said it wasn't right. John said Jesus should baptize him. But Jesus persuaded him, and when Jesus was baptized, God said, "This is my dear Son. I am very pleased with Him."

Dear God, help me to turn away from sin and follow Jesus. Amen.

A New Job for Matthew

(Mark 2:14-17)

Matthew was one of God's people. He worked for the Romans as a tax official. Some tax men were liars. They wanted to get rich, so they took too much money from people.

So Matthew gave a party for his friends.
Jesus was the guest of honor. And some of
Matthew's friends decided to follow Jesus.

*Dear God, help me to tell my friends about
Jesus just as Matthew did. Amen.*

A Roman Commander Has Faith

(Matthew 8:5-13)

A Roman army officer heard about Jesus. He heard about the wonderful things Jesus did. One day the officer's helper became very sick. His helper was about to die. So the Roman officer went to see Jesus. He asked Jesus to make his helper well.

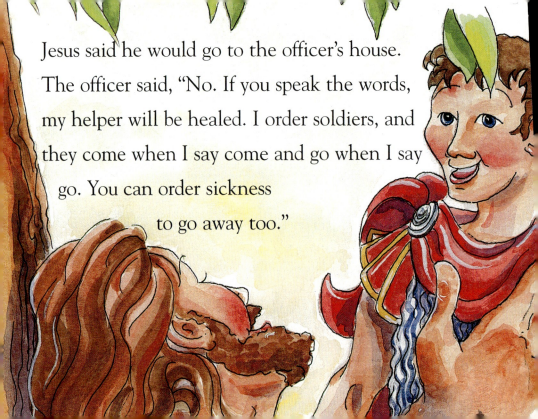

Jesus said he would go to the officer's house. The officer said, "No. If you speak the words, my helper will be healed. I order soldiers, and they come when I say come and go when I say go. You can order sickness to go away too."

When Jesus heard the officer's words, He was amazed. Jesus said, "You have great faith. Your helper will not die." And the helper was healed immediately.

*Dear God, You can do anything!
Help me to have great faith too. Amen.*

A Boy Gives His Lunch Away

(John 6:1-15)

One day many people followed Jesus into the hills. He taught them and made sick people well. When suppertime came, thousands of people were still there. They were hungry too. Jesus told His disciples to feed them.

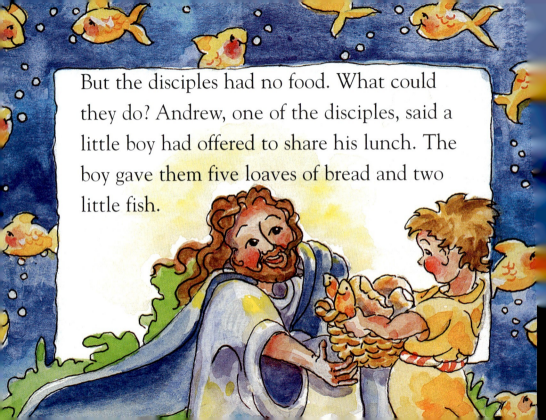

But the disciples had no food. What could they do? Andrew, one of the disciples, said a little boy had offered to share his lunch. The boy gave them five loaves of bread and two little fish.

Jesus gave thanks to God. Then Jesus broke the boy's lunch into pieces. The disciples gave food to everyone. No one went hungry. It was a miracle!

Thank You, Lord, for the boy who shared his lunch. Help me to share my things too. Amen.

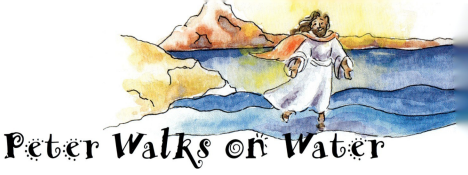

Peter Walks on Water

(Matthew 14:22-36)

Peter and the disciples went out on the sea in their boat. But a big storm came, and the boat began to sink. The disciples yelled for help. Jesus came towards them. He was walking on the water. They were scared!

Jesus said, "Don't be afraid. It is I." Peter saw Him and said, "If that is really You, Lord, tell me to come to You." And Jesus said, "Come!" So Peter stepped out of the boat and started to walk on the water too.

Then Peter saw the waves. He felt the wind. Peter began to sink. "Help me, Lord!" he cried. So Jesus reached out and saved him.

Thank You, Lord, that You always hear my prayers and save me too. Amen.

A Brave Believer

(Acts 6–7)

After Jesus went back to heaven, the disciples went from city to city telling people about Him. Stephen told wonderful stories about Jesus. He did miracles in Jesus' name too. But Stephen's words about Jesus made some people angry.

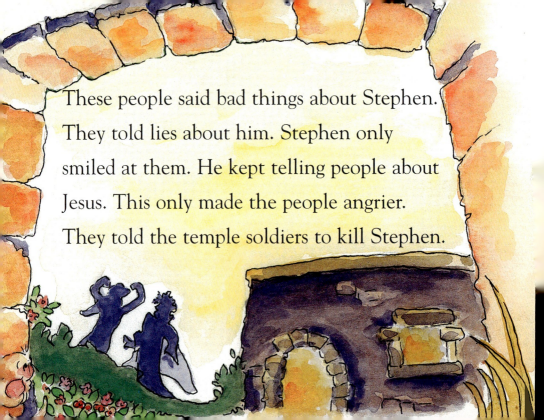

These people said bad things about Stephen. They told lies about him. Stephen only smiled at them. He kept telling people about Jesus. This only made the people angrier. They told the temple soldiers to kill Stephen.

Stephen was brave. As the soldiers took him away, Stephen smiled. He asked God to forgive everyone who was angry with him.

Dear God, help me to be brave like Stephen when I tell others about Jesus. Amen.

You Can Stay with Us

(Acts 18:1-19)

Paul went to a city called Corinth to tell people about Jesus. He met a man named Aquila. Aquila's wife was named Priscilla. Aquila and Priscilla knew how to make tents. Paul knew how to make tents too.

So Aquila and Priscilla became Paul's friends. They told Paul he could stay at their house. During the day, they all made tents. Paul taught people about Jesus everywhere he went.

Paul stayed with Aquila and Priscilla for more than a year. And many people in Corinth learned about Jesus.

Thank You, God, for Aquila and Priscilla's friendship with Paul. Help me to be a friend too. Amen.

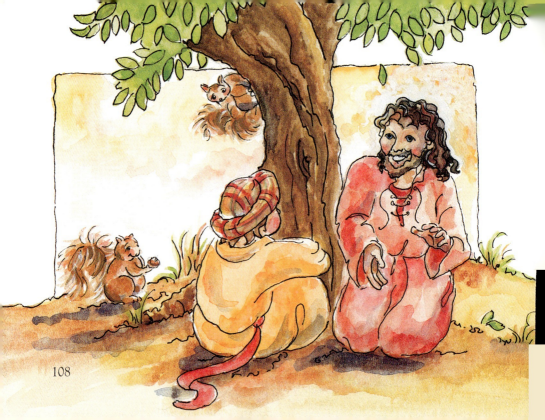

Just Like a Son

(1 Corinthians 4:17; 1 Timothy 1:18; 2 Timothy 1-7)

When Timothy was a little boy, Paul told him about Jesus. Paul showed Timothy how to live like Jesus. When Timothy grew up, he went with Paul to other cities. He told people about Jesus too.

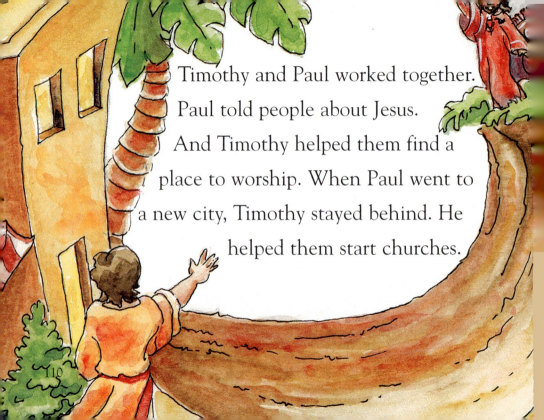

Timothy and Paul worked together. Paul told people about Jesus. And Timothy helped them find a place to worship. When Paul went to a new city, Timothy stayed behind. He helped them start churches.

Timothy helped Paul when Paul went to prison for telling people about Jesus. Paul said Timothy was like a son to him.

Dear God, help me to be a willing helper like Timothy. Amen.

If you have enjoyed this book, or if it has
impacted your life, we would like to hear from you.
Please contact us at:

Honor Books
Department E
P.O. Box 55388
Tulsa, Oklahoma 74155
Or by e-mail at info@honorbooks.com

Additional copies of this book and other titles
in the *God's Little Story Book* series
are available from your local bookstore.